THE MOON
ON THE
ONE HAND

WILLIAM CROFUT

THE MOON ON THE ONE HAND

Poetry In Song

ARRANGEMENTS BY

Kenneth Cooper & Glenn Shattuck

ILLUSTRATIONS BY

Susan Crofut

A Margaret K. McElderry Book

Atheneum   1975   New York

A recording of the songs in the book is available from
William Crofut, Spectacle Lane, Wilton, Connecticut 06897.

Library of Congress Cataloging in Publication Data
Crofut, Bill. The moon on the one hand.
"A Margaret K. McElderry book."
SUMMARY: *A collection of poems set to music,*
mostly about animals and nature, by Robert
Louis Stevenson, Randall Jarrell, James
Stephens, e. e. cummings, and other poets.
1. Children's songs. [*1. Songs. 2. Poetry—Collections. 3. Nature—Poetry*] *I. Crofut, Susan, ill.*
II. Title.
M1997.C947M6   784.6   74-18179
ISBN *0-689-50018-1*

Published simultaneously in Canada by
McClelland & Stewart, Ltd.
Manufactured in the United States of America by
Halliday Lithograph Corporation, West Hanover, Massachusetts
Designed by Harriett Barton
First Edition

To Erika & Anni

Hilaire Belloc, "The Early Morning" from
Sonnets and Verse, *reprinted by permission of A D Peters
and Company. e.e. cummings, "in Just" copyright, 1923,
1951 by e.e. cummings. From his volume* Complete Poems
1913-1962 *by permission of Harcourt Brace Jovanovich.
Elizabeth Flemming, "Who's In" reprinted by permission
of Blackie & Son Limited. Randall Jarrell, "The Bird of
Night," "The Chipmunk's Day," and "The Mockingbird"
reprinted with permission of Macmillan Publishing Co., Inc.
from* The Bat-Poet *by Randall Jarrell. Copyright ©
Macmillan Publishing Co., Inc., 1963, 1964.
Laura E. Richards, "Eletelephony" from* Tirra Lirra,
*copyright, 1935 by Laura E. Richards. Copyright, 1955 by
Little, Brown and Company. James Stephens, "The Goat
Paths" and "White Fields" reprinted by permission of
the Society of Authors as the literary representative
of the Estate of James Stephens.*

ACKNOWLEDGMENTS

Robert Penn Warren, his wife Eleanor Clark, and Peter and Anne Prescott introduced me to most of the poetry and listened, criticized and encouraged as the songs grew. Chris Brubeck helped with some of the piano arrangements. John Guth assisted with the guitar arrangements. A. D. Peters & Company has been most generous in granting us permission to use the first line of Hilaire Belloc's poem "The Early Morning" as the title for this book.

Audrey Hartman of Columbia Artists Management has given nearly a decade of untiring loyalty and support without which this project would never have been possible. And most of all special thanks go to my wife and parents for their patience and help over the years.

Contents

Bill Crofut's Foreword

In 1967, a friend sent me an anonymous nursery rhyme, "A Man of Words," with a note suggesting I set the poem to music. In writing the music for it (my first song), I realized the marvelous possibilities of using great verse in song. This is not a new idea—after all, Beethoven and Schubert took it for granted—but for me it was a fresh approach.

The selection of poetry for this song collection was based on a desire to share, with my own children, poetry I was reading for the first time (James Stephens, Randall Jarrell, John Clare) as well as poems I had known as a child, such as "The Cow" and "The Wind" by Robert Louis Stevenson. The idea worked so well that the children began bringing books of poetry home from the library to look for new ideas to suggest for songs. And somehow the songs kept coming.

Most of the poetry is about animals and nature. We live beside a swamp that attracts many kinds of birds (including ducks and Canadian geese), red fox, deer, and large turtles that bask in the sun on the Connecticut rock outcroppings. Our house is filled with pets, ranging from the usual domestic animals to stray wild creatures that are nursed with baby bottles and eyedroppers, too often without success. Having lived with these animals and witnessed their habits firsthand—sometimes even having participated in their life cycles by delivering their kittens, puppies, or calves—the children have developed strong feelings for their character and their dignity. I have, therefore, carefully avoided any musical idiom that might in any way even suggest caricature.

Sometimes the music follows the action of the words, such as the dissonance of the thunderbolt in Tennyson's "The Eagle," but more often it rings of nostalgia for a world that is vanishing, as in Stevenson's "The Cow." The song was written in Austria. On a farm next to our house there, the cows never left their barn to graze in the beautiful Alpine meadows. The grass was brought to them, and in their lifetime they were never "blown by all the winds that pass," or "wet with all the showers." The melancholy quality of the music reflects the loss of the untouched nature everyone took for granted in the last century.

The selection of poetry represents dreams and realities that are still a part of our life—goat paths, chipmunks, mockingbirds and kites—a timeless world, threatened on many fronts, that might so easily vanish forever from our lives.

Ken Cooper's Foreword

The songs in this collection represent an unusual blend of elements: fine poetry set in a folk style and arranged for children and young adults to sing and play. Bill Crofut, Glenn Shattuck and I have tried to combine ease and pleasure with challenge and stimulation for people young and old who have limited musical experience, but unlimited curiosity. Some of the songs are singable and playable almost at sight—"The Wind," "Little Trotty Wagtail," and "Child's Song"—while others will take some putting together—"The Goat Paths," "A Man of Words," and, especially "The Chipmunk's Day." Everything has been figured out so that *if you pull it apart* into elements that are easy to grasp, *you will be able to put it together.* There are rewards: once learned, the songs will begin to grow on you, and you will enjoy singing them again and again, perhaps in different ways. I know you will find that "The Chipmunk's Day," sung really fast, is one of the most captivating songs in the English language.

Rather than have all the arrangements in the same style, we have thought to include a variety of styles and a variety of instrumental possibilities. There are old-fashioned piano styles that conjure up the nostalgia Bill was talking about, and there are slightly spicy, newer keyboard styles that might be particularly effective on the harpsichord. There are *obbligato* parts for recorders, which can, of course, be played on flutes, violins, harmonicas, or anything else that will play the notes, or they can be sung to the words of the song. Nothing is very difficult, but some organization may be necessary. And there are guitar chords that can be regarded as an invitation to make up some interesting accompanying figuration, in the character of the song.

In short, the point of the arrangements is to promote your enjoyment of the poems and the songs—and of the birds and animals they sing about.

THE MOON
ON THE
ONE HAND

THE WIND

Robert Louis Stevenson

I saw you toss the kites on high
And blow the birds about the sky;
And all around I heard you pass,
Like ladies' skirts across the grass—
    O wind, a-blowing all day long,
    O wind, that sings so loud a song!

I saw the different things you did,
But always you yourself you hid.
I felt you push, I heard you call,
I could not see yourself at all—
    O wind, a-blowing all day long,
    O wind, that sings so loud a song!

O you that are so strong and cold,
O blower, are you young or old?
Are you a beast of field and tree,
Or just a stronger child than me?
    O wind, a-blowing all day long,
    O wind, that sings so loud a song!

THE WIND

Poem by Robert Louis Stevenson

Music by Bill Crofut
Arrangement by Kenneth Cooper

1. I saw you toss_____ the
2. I saw the diff - erent
3. O you that are_____ so

kites on high_____ And blow the birds_____ a -
things you did,_____ But al - ways you_____ your -
strong and cold,_____ O blow - er, are_____ you

all day long, O wind, that sings so loud _____ a song! _____

6

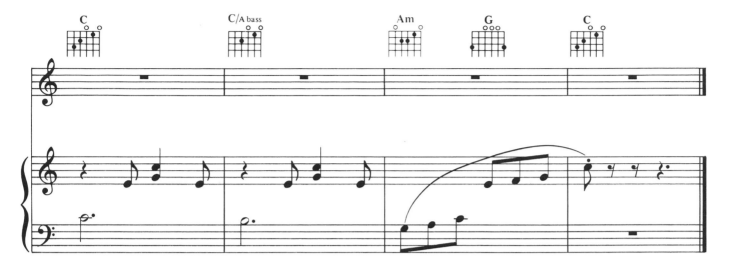

LITTLE TROTTY WAGTAIL

John Clare

Little trotty wagtail, he went in the rain,
And tittering, tottering sideways he ne'er got straight again.
He stooped to get a worm, and looked up to get a fly,
And then he flew away ere his feathers they were dry.

Little trotty wagtail, he waddled in the mud,
And left his little footmarks, trample where he would.
He waddled in the water-pudge, and waggle went his tail,
And chirrupt up his wings to dry upon the garden rail.

Little trotty wagtail, you nimble all about,
And in the dimpling water-pudge you waddle in and out;
Your home is nigh at hand, and in the warm pigsty.
So, little Master Wagtail, I'll bid you a good-bye.

LITTLE TROTTY WAGTAIL

Poem by John Clare

Music by Bill Crofut
Arrangement by Kenneth Cooper

1. Lit - tle trot - ty wag - tail,__ he went in the__ rain, And
2. Lit - tle trot - ty wag - tail,__ he wad - dled in the mud, And
3. Lit - tle trot - ty wag - tail,__ you nim - ble all a - bout, And

titter - ing, totter - ing side - ways__ he ne'er got straight a - gain. He
left his lit - tle foot - marks_____ tram - ple where he would. He
in the dimp - ling water - pudge you wad - dle in and out; Your

stooped to get a worm,___ and looked up to get a fly, And
wad - dled in the wat - er - pudge, and wag - gle went his tail. And
home is nigh at hand,___ and___ in the warm pig sty. So,

then he flew a - way ere___ his feath - ers they were dry.
chir - rupt up his wings to dry up - on the gar - den rail.
lit - tle Mas - ter Wag___ tail I'll bid you a good - by.

THE COW

Robert Louis Stevenson

The friendly cow all red and white,
　　I love with all my heart:
She gives me cream, with all her might,
　　To eat with apple-tart.

She wanders lowing here and there,
　　And yet she cannot stray,
All in the pleasant open air,
　　The pleasant light of day:

And blown by all the winds that pass
　　And wet with all the showers,
She walks among the meadow grass
　　And eats the meadow flowers.

THE COW

Poem by Robert Louis Stevenson

Music by Bill Crofut
Arrangement by Glenn Shattuck

1. The friend - ly cow all red and white, I love with all my
2. She wan - ders low - ing here and there, And yet she can - not

heart:
stray,

She gives me cream, with all her might,
All in the pleas - ant o - pen air,

To eat with ap - ple - tart.
The pleas - ant light of

day:

And blown by all the winds that pass

And wet with all the

15

showers,   She walks   a - mong   the   mead - ow   grass

And   eats   the   mead - ow   flowers.

THE EARLY MORNING

Hilaire Belloc

The moon on the one hand, the dawn on the other:
The moon is my sister, the dawn is my brother.
The moon on my left, the dawn on my right
My brother, good morning: my sister, good night.

THE EARLY MORNING

Poem by Hilaire Belloc

Music by Bill Crofut
Arrangement by Glenn Shattuck

18

sis - ter,_ the dawn is my bro-ther. The moon on my left,___ the

dawn on my right___ My bro-ther, good morn - ing:___ my

sis - ter, good night.___

ritardando

19

IN JUST

e.e. cummings

in Just-
spring   when the world is mud-
luscious the little
lame balloonman

whistles   far   and wee

and eddieandbill come
running from marbles and
piracies and it's
spring

when the world is puddle-wonderful

the queer
old balloonman whistles
far   and   wee
and bettyandisbel come dancing

from hop-scotch and jump-rope and

it's
spring
and
      the

            goat-footed

balloonMan   whistles
far
and
wee

IN JUST

Poem by e.e. cummings

Music by Bill Crofut
Arrangement by Glenn Shattuck

in Just - spring when the world is mud - lus - cious the

lit - tle lame bal - loon-man whis - tles far and wee

and ed - die - and - bill come run - ning from

and bet - ty - and - is - bel come
danc - ing from hop - scotch and jump - rope and it's spring and the
goat - foot - ed bal - loon - Man whis - tles far and wee

WHITE FIELDS

James Stephens

In the wintertime we go
Walking in the fields of snow;

Where there is no grass at all;
Where the top of every wall,

Every fence and every tree,
Is as white as white can be.

Pointing out the way we came,
—Every one of them the same—

All across the fields there be
Prints in silver filigree;

And our mothers always know,
By the footprints in the snow,

Where it is the children go.

WHITE FIELDS

Poem by James Stephens

Music by Bill Crofut
Arrangement by Glenn Shattuck

1. In the win - ter - time we go   Walk - ing in the
2. In the win - ter - time we go   Walk - ing in the

fields of snow;   Where there is   no   grass   at   all;
fields of snow;   Point - ing   out   the   way   we   came,

27

al - ways know, By the foot - prints in the snow,
al - ways know, By the foot - prints in the snow,

Where it is the child - ren 1. go.
Where it is the child - ren

1. C

2. C
2. go.

slowly

THE CHIPMUNK'S DAY

Randall Jarrell

In and out the bushes, up the ivy,
Into the hole
By the old oak stump, the chipmunk flashes.
Up the pole

To the feeder full of seeds he dashes,
Stuffs his cheeks,
The chickadee and titmouse scold him.
Down he streaks.

Red as the leaves the wind blows off the maple,
Red as a fox,
Striped like a skunk, the chipmunk whistles
Past the love seat, past the mailbox,

Down the path,
Home to his warm hole stuffed with sweet
Things to eat.
Neat and slight and shining, his front feet

Curled at his breast, he sits there while the sun
Stripes the red west
With its last light: the chipmunk
Dives to his rest.

THE CHIPMUNK'S DAY

Poem by Randall Jarrell

Music by Bill Crofut
Arrangement by Kenneth Cooper

30

THE MOCKINGBIRD

Randall Jarrell

Look one way and the sun is going down,
Look the other and the moon is rising.
The sparrow's shadow's longer than the lawn.
The bats squeak: "Night is here"; the birds cheep: "Day is gone."
On the willow's highest branch, monopolizing
Day and night, cheeping, squeaking, soaring,
The mockingbird is imitating life.

All day the mockingbird has owned the yard.
As light first woke the world, the sparrows trooped
Onto the seedy lawn: the mockingbird
Chased them off shrieking. Hour by hour, fighting hard
To make the world his own, he swooped
On thrushes, thrashers, jays and chickadees—
At noon he drove away a big black cat.

Now, in the moonlight, he sits here and sings.
A thrush is singing, then a thrasher, then a jay—
Then all at once, a cat begins meowing.
A mockingbird can sound like anything.
He imitates the world he drove away
So well that for a minute, in the moonlight,
Which one's the mockingbird? Which one's the world?

THE MOCKINGBIRD

Poem by Randall Jarrell

Music by Bill Crofut
Arranged by Glenn Shattuck

Look one way, the sun is go-ing down, Look the oth-er and the moon is

ris - ing. _____ The spar-row's sha-dow's

long-er than the lawn.___ The bats squeak:"Night is here;" the

birds cheep:"Day is gone." On the wil-low's high-est branch,___ mon-o-po-

liz-ing_____ Day and night, cheep-ing, squeak-ing,

seed-y lawn:— the mock-ing-bird— chased them off shriek-ing.

Hour by hour, fight-ing hard To make the world his own,— he

swooped On thrush-es, thrash-ers, jays, and chick-a-dees—

37

38

Now, in the moon - light, he sits___ here and sings. A

thrush is sing - ing, then a thrash - er, then a jay— Then

39

all at once, a cat be - gins me - ow - ing.___ A mock - ing - bird can

sound like an - y - thing. He im - i - tates the world he drove a -

way So well that for a min - ute,_____ in the

41

THE BIRD OF NIGHT

Randall Jarrell

A shadow is floating through the moonlight,
Its wings don't make a sound.
Its claws are long, its beak is bright.
Its eyes try all the corners of the night.

It calls and calls: all the air swells and heaves
And washes up and down like water.
The ear that listens to the owl believes
In death. The bat beneath the eaves,

The mouse beside the stone are still as death.
The owl's air washes them like water.
The owl goes back and forth inside the night,
And the night holds its breath.

THE BIRD OF NIGHT

Poem by Randall Jarrell

Music by Bill Crofut
Arranged by Glenn Shattuck

A shad-ow is float-ing through the moon-light. Its

wings don't make a sound. Its claws are long, its beak is bright. Its

eyes____ try all the cor-ners____ of the night.____ It

calls and calls: all the air swells and heaves And wash-es up and down like

wa - ter. The ear that lis-tens to the owl be-lieves In

death. The bat be-neath the eaves, The mouse be-side the stone are

still as death. The owl's air wash-es them like wa - ter. The

owl goes back and forth_____ in - side the night, And the

night holds its breath.

THE EAGLE

Alfred, Lord Tennyson

He clasps the crag with crooked hands;
Close to the sun in lonely lands,
Ringed with the azure world, he stands.

The wrinkled sea beneath him crawls;
He watches from his mountain walls,
and like a thunderbolt he falls.

THE EAGLE

Poem by Alfred, Lord Tennyson

Music by Bill Crofut
Arrangement by Glenn Shattuck

He clasps___ the crag___ with crook-ed___ hands;

49

THE GOAT PATHS

James Stephens

The crooked paths go every way
Upon the hill—they wind about
Through the heather in and out
Of the quiet sunniness.
And there the goats, day after day,

Stray in sunny quietness,
Cropping here and cropping there,
As they pause and turn and pass,
Now a bit of heather spray
Now a mouthful of the grass.

In the deeper sunniness,
In the place where nothing stirs,
Quietly in quietness,
In the quiet of the furze,
For a time they come and lie
Staring on the roving sky.

If you approach they run away,
They leap and stare, away they bound,
With a sudden angry sound,
to the sunny quietude;
Crouching down where nothing stirs
In the silence of the furze,
Crouching down again to brood
In the sunny solitude.

If I were as wise as they
I would stray apart and brood,
I would beat a hidden way
Through the quiet heather spray
To a sunny solitude;

And should you come I'd run away,
I would make an angry sound,
I would stare and turn and bound
To the deeper quietude,
To the place where nothing stirs
In the silence of the furze.

In that airy quietness
I would think as long as they;
Through the quiet sunniness
I would stray away to brood
By a hidden, beaten way
In the sunny solitude,

I would think until I found
Something I can never find,
Something lying on the ground,
In the bottom of my mind.

THE GOAT PATHS

Poem by James Stephens

Music by Bill Crofut
Arranged by Glenn Shattuck

The crook-ed paths go ev-ery way__ Up-on the hill they wind a-bout__ Through the hea-ther in and out Of the qui-et_____ sun-ni-ness. And there the goats, day_____

on the   ground, In the bot - tom   of   my   mind.

ELETELEPHONY

Laura Richards

Once there was an elephant
Who tried to use the telephant
No No I mean an elephone
Who tried to use the telephone
(Dear me I am not certain quite
That even now I've got it right)

However it was he got his trunk
Entangled in a telephunk
The more he tried to get it free
The louder buzzed the telephee
(I fear I'd better drop the song
Of elephop and telephong)

ELETELEPHONY

Poem by Laura Richards

Music by Bill Crofut
Arranged by Glenn Shattuck

Once there was an el-e-phant Who tried to use the tel-e-phant No

No I mean an el-e-phone who tried to use the tel-e-phone (Dear

me I am not cer-tain quite That e-ven now I've got it right)

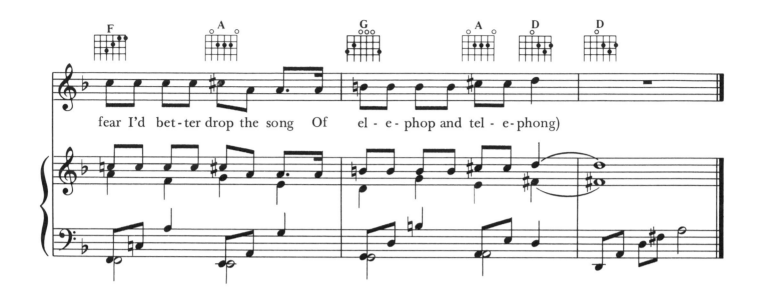

fear I'd bet-ter drop the song Of el - e - phop and tel - e - phong)

WHO'S IN

Elizabeth Fleming

"The door is shut fast
  And everyone's out."
  But people don't know what they're talking about!
  Say the fly on the wall,
  And the flame on the coals,
  And the dog on his rug,
  And the mice in their holes,
  And the kitten curled up,
  And the spiders that spin—
"What, everyone out?
  Why, everyone's in!"

WHO'S IN

Poem by Elizabeth Fleming

Music by Bill Crofut
Arrangement by Kenneth Cooper

Fast and whispered, like a secret

"The door is shut fast and ev-er-y-one's out." But the peo-ple don't know what they're talk-ing a-bout! Say the fly on the wall, And the flame on the coals, And the dog on his rug, And the mice in their holes, And the

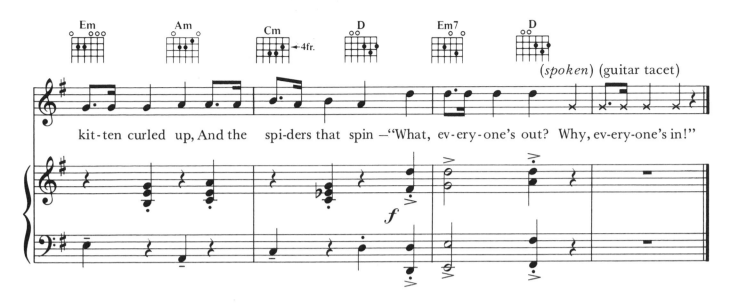

(spoken) (guitar tacet)

kit-ten curled up, And the spi-ders that spin —"What, ev-ery-one's out? Why, ev-ery-one's in!"

f

A MAN OF WORDS

Anonymous

A man of words and not of deeds,
Is like a garden full of weeds;

And when the weeds begin to grow,
It's like a garden full of snow;

And when the snow begins to fall,
It is like birds upon a wall;

And when the birds begin to fly,
It's like a shipwreck in the sky;

And when the sky begins to roar,
It's like a lion at the door;

And when the door begins to crack,
It's like a stick across your back;

And when your back begins to smart,
It's like a penknife in your heart;

And when your heart begins to bleed,
Oh then you're dead and dead indeed!

A MAN OF WORDS

Anonymous Poet

Music by Bill Crofut
Arrangement by Kenneth Cooper

Slow, but two pulses to a measure

1. A man of words and not of deeds, Is like a gar-den full of weeds; And when the weeds be-gin to grow, It's like a gar-den full of
2. And when the snow be-gins to fall, It is like birds u-pon a wall; And when the birds be-gin to fly, It's like a ship-wreck in the

snow;
sky;

Three recorders

Small drum

3. And when the sky be - gins to roar, It's like a
4. And when your back be - gins to smart, It's like a

li - on at the door; And when the door be - gins to
pen - knife in your heart; And when your heart be - gins to

crack, It's like a stick a - cross your back; *pp*
bleed, Oh then you're dead and dead in - deed!

Three recorders

Small drum

73

5. A man of words and not of deeds, Is like a gar - den full of

weeds; And when the weeds be-gin to grow, It's like a gar-den full of snow.

CHILD'S SONG

Thomas Moore

I have a garden of my own,
  Shining with flowers of every hue;
I love it dearly while alone,
  But I shall love it more with you:
And there the golden bees shall crone,
  In summertime at break of morn,
And wake us with their busy hum
  Around the Siha's fragrant thorn.

I have a fawn from Aden's land,
  On leafy buds and berries nurst;
And you shall feed him from your hand,
  Though he may start with fear at first.
And I will lead you where he lies
  For shelter in the noon-tide heat;
And you may touch his sleepy eyes,
  And feel his little silvery feet.

CHILD'S SONG

Poem by Thomas Moore

Music by Bill Crofut
Arrangement by Kenneth Cooper

78

Shin-ing with flow-ers of ev-ery hue;_____ I love it dear-ly

while a-lone,__ But I shall love it more with you.__